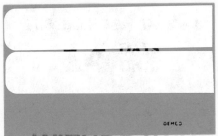
DATE DUE

GAYLORD			PRINTED IN U.S.A

LOOK AT
WHOOPS,
WORDS,
AND WHISTLES

© Franklin Watts Inc.

Franklin Watts
387 Park Avenue South
New York
N.Y. 10016

Library of Congress Cataloging-in-Publication Data
Pluckrose, Henry Arthur.
    Whoops, words, and whistles / Henry Pluckrose.
        p.   cm. — (Look at)
    Summary: Examines forms of animal communication, including warning
signals, family communication, and mating calls.
    ISBN 0-531-14047-4
        1. Animal communication—Juvenile literature. [1. Animal
communication.] I. Title.
    QL776.P58   1990   90-12195
    591.59—dc20   CIP AC

Editor: Kate Petty
Design Concept: David Bennett

Phototypeset by Lineage Ltd, Watford
Printed in Italy by G. Canale & C.S.p.A. – Turin

Additional photographs: H Angel 22; Ardea 8l, 17t, 23, 26c; Camera Press 4b;
Chris Fairclough Colour Library 4t, 5t, 7, 9b, 10 (both), 25r, 29r;
D and E Hosking 24l; Hutchison Library 5b, 6; Natural History Photographic
Agency 11, 12, 13, 16, 17c, 20, 24r, 25l, 28r, 29l; Oxford Scientific Films 18, 26t;
Planet Earth Pictures 15, 17b, 21; Survival Anglia 9t, 14tr, 19, 26b, 27tr; ZEFA 8r,
14b, 27b, 28l.

Front cover: Ardea

LOOK AT
WHOOPS,
WORDS,
AND
WHISTLES

Henry Pluckrose

FRANKLIN WATTS

New York • London • Sydney • Toronto

We communicate
in many ways.
Sometimes we just use signs.

More often we use sounds.
The sounds we make are usually words.
Each word has a particular meaning.

Not everyone will understand our words.
Each different language has its own words.

Sometimes we show how we feel
by making noises, rather than words.

Animals also use sounds to communicate.
They make sounds to keep in contact with
other members of the family.
The chick chirps when it is ready
to come out of the egg.

Sounds that are too high-pitched for humans to hear are called ultrasonic or ultrasounds.

Shrew

Housemice

Many animals that live underground make high-pitched sounds. Their enemies cannot hear these sounds through the earth.

African elephants

Sounds that are too low for us to hear
are called infrasonic or infrasounds.
The elephant can make a low rumble in its
chest. Other elephants hear the rumble.
A human being cannot hear it.

How do we know animals can hear sounds
that we cannot hear?

A sheepdog follows directions given by
the shepherd's high-pitched whistle.
The shepherd hears nothing.

Long-eared bat

Bats make ultrasounds.
As it flies, the European bat makes a
high-pitched "click." Its big ears pick
up the echo from its own call, helping
the bat to find its way in the dark.

Bats use echoes as they hunt for insects. The echo tells the bat where the insect is, even though it can't see it.

Long-eared bat

Moths are hunted by bats. The tiger moth
makes its own high-pitched sound to warn
hungry bats that it is unpleasant to eat.
Some creatures use sound for protection.

Like us, animals live in a world of many sounds. Like us, they can identify very slight differences in sound. The Adelie penguin can recognize her chick's voice — even when the beach is crowded.

The Indian langur monkey has a special
cry to warn of danger.
If a hawk flies too near, the monkey waves
its arms and screams.

Most creatures try to control the territory
in which they live.
The male English robin sings to warn all
other robins that the land belongs to him!

Some creatures make a warning sound only when they are angry.

The puff adder hisses.

The rattlesnake rattles.

Puff adder

Prairie rattlesnake

The Indian rat snake makes a gentle hum.

Indian rat snake

The gorillas of central Africa do not need
to make noises to frighten away enemies.
They live together in families and
communicate in quiet grunts and gurgles.

The orangutan of Borneo makes quiet noises. Its calls include grunts, sighs, hoots, and squeaks.

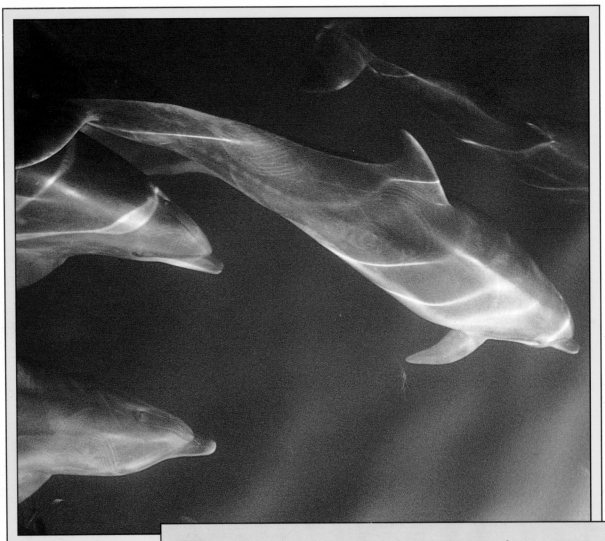

Sea mammals make sounds under water. Dolphins have over twenty different calls. Like bats, dolphins use echoes to build up a picture of what is happening in the sea around them.

During the calving season, humpback whales gather off the coast of Hawaii.
They sing in chorus – a mixture of yelps, growls, squeaks, rumbles, and squeals.
The singing helps keep the group together.

Sound travels easily through water.

The catfish can make a sound like
the beating of a drum by vibrating a special
muscle near its swim bladder.

The haddock makes a purring sound.

Blackbird

Chaffinch

Cries and calls are used to find a mate.
Birds whose coloring is dull
often have the most complicated songs.

Birds that live in open countryside often have bright plumage.

Peacock

Pheasant

They attract their mates with beautiful feathers, though their cries can be rather harsh and boring.

Lapwing

Some birds "sing" as they fly.

Skylarks sing *only* when they are in flight.

Skylark

Geese often "honk" as they fly from one feeding place to the next.

Geese

26

Some animals make sounds in unusual ways.
Frogs and toads make their voices louder
by extending their throats.

Square marked toad

Bush cricket

The male cricket makes a noise to attract
its mate by rubbing its wings together.

The sounds they make give some creatures
their names.
The gecko lizard of south-east Asia
is called the "Tokay."

Tokay gecko

Trumpeter cranes

The South American crane is called the
"Trumpeter."

Although we cannot understand all the sounds animals make, here are some that we know the meaning of...

the dog's growl

the cat's purr.

How many more examples can you think of?

Did you know?

● Sound travels in waves. Very high-pitched sounds are outside the range of human hearing. At best, a human being can hear sound waves of 20,000 vibrations in one second. A fruit bat can produce and hear sound waves of between 50,000 and 200,000 vibrations in one second.

● The dolphin can produce sound waves that travel through water at 200,000 vibrations per second. The sound is produced by the larynx (throat) and a special organ (called a melon) in the front of the dolphin's head. Dolphins use the sounds they make to catch food. They can make such a loud burst of noise that the fishes they are hunting are confused by the sounds and so become easier to catch.

● Sound travels at a speed of 1105 feet (340m) through air. Sound travels five times as fast as this through water.

Have you noticed...?

● When an ambulance or police car is moving towards you at speed, the siren seems to have a very high pitch. This is because the sound waves moving towards you have become tightly bunched. When the vehicle has passed, the siren seems to change its note and become lower. This is because the sound waves are no longer bunched.

Something to do

● Make lists of the calls and sounds made by animals and birds.

Animal/Bird	Sound
cow	moooo
duck	quack
cat	miaow
frog	croak
horse	neigh

Listening

● Put a watch to your ear. Listen to its ticking. The sound waves made by the ticking cause your ear drum to vibrate. Now hold the watch firmly between your teeth and cover your ears with your hands.

Can you still hear the watch?
Is the ticking louder or softer than it was before?
How are the sound waves managing to reach your ear drums?

● Stand in a playground, garden or open space.
How many different kinds of sound can you hear?
Can you guess how each sound is made?

Words describing animal sounds

bark	chirrup	hiss	roar	warble
bellow	click	honk	scream	whimper
boom	cluck	hoot	shriek	whinny
bray	croak	howl	sing	whistle
buzz	croon	hum	snarl	whoop
call	crow	mew	squawk	yap
caterwaul	cry	miaow	squeak	yelp
chatter	drone	neigh	squeal	yowl
cheep	growl	purr	tweet	
chirp	grunt	quack	twitter	

Index